Decision Making in Educational Settings

by
Charles C. Sharman

Library of Congress Catalog Card Number 84-61205
ISBN 0-87367-211-9

This fastback is sponsored by the Arizona State University Chapter of Phi Delta Kappa, which made a generous contribution toward publication costs.

The chapter sponsors this fastback to honor Arizona State University's "Century of Excellence," 1885 - 1985.

Table of Contents

Table of Contents

Introduction

Decision making is an activity in which all humans expend a considerable amount of their time and energy. It is probably fair to say that the degree of success an individual, group, or organization experiences over a given period of time is directly proportional to the quality of the decisions they make during that period of time. While decision making occurs in both personal and organizational settings, the material included in this fastback will focus on decision making in formal organizations, particularly education organizations.

Decision making in organizational settings has been thought of by most people as an activity performed by formal leaders in hierarchical ways. For example, in most education organizations decision making was traditionally considered to be the prerogative of the school administration. However, in recent years considerable evidence has supported the idea that all members of an organization, not only formal leaders, contribute to the quality of the decisions made in an organization.

This fastback will review decision making from the perspective of school teachers and other educators.

Thinking About Decision Making

Consider a decision-making situation near and dear to all of us, the committee. Place yourself in the following hypothetical situation.

You have just been named chairperson of a blue-ribbon committee for your school, Happy Daze Elementary. The committee is a very important one. The decisions it reaches during the coming year will have significant impact on the school's administration, teachers, parents, and students.

Happy Daze is a large elementary school with 850 pupils, 3 administrators, 35 teachers, and 7 other staff members. You have been a teacher at Happy Daze for eight years and have been a grade-level chairperson for the last three years. While serving at Happy Daze, you have become one of the most influential people in the school and community; that is the primary reason you have been named chairperson of this powerful committee. Your nine-member committee is composed of one assistant administrator, two teachers, and five parents.

It is early September, and you have been given a deadline of March 15 to submit your final report. Consider the following situations and choose the best response for each situation.

1. It is September 20, and this is the first meeting of your committee. You are very aware of the amount of work that must be completed by March 15.

    A. You tell the committee you want all work completed by February 15. This gives you a reasonable time cushion.

    B. Don't mention time lines at this time. It is your feeling that it would be better to approach the topic of time after you have had several meetings and have begun to know one another better.

C. Tell the committee how important you think time lines are for completing various elements of the project, and tell them you need their help in establishing realistic time lines.

D. Tell the committee when you need various elements of the project completed and when the final report must be finished.

2. It is your third meeting, and during previous deliberations your committee decided that one of its most important jobs was to establish some policies concerning school discipline. In fact, they decided they wanted to devote their next several meetings to this topic. You will not be able to attend those meetings because of other unavoidable commitments. You decide to:

A. Let the committee work alone and establish some basic discipline policies.

B. Let the committee establish some preliminary policies with the understanding that no final decisions will be made until you return.

C. Arrange for the school's principal to take your place and guide the committee while you are gone.

D. Instruct the committee to work on less controversial issues while you are gone.

3. When you return and meet with the group, you find that the committee has divided itself into three subgroups and that each subgroup has developed a set of policies that conflict with those developed by the other subgroups. Furthermore, each subgroup is pressuring you to support its recommendations and is unwilling to consider realistically the recommendations of the other subgroups. You decide that the best way to deal with this situation is to:

A. Select the recommendations that you feel would be most constructive.

B. Have the entire committee vote on the recommendations of each subgroup with the recommendations receiving the most votes being the ones selected.

C. Have the entire faculty vote on the recommendations of the three subgroups.

D. Ask the entire committee to meet with you and deliberate further.

4. It is December and your committee is not being very productive. To make matters worse, they are not responding very well to your "polite prodding." You decide to:

A. Have them meet without you for a while in order to have a chance to work things out alone.

B. Really get on the committee's case. Remind them of the approaching deadlines.

C. Talk with the individual members of the committee to identify specific problems and suggestions for dealing with them.

D. Tell the committee you don't know what the problem is, but you are willing to resign if that will help.

5. It is getting close to your deadline, and three of the most influential members of your committee informed you that they need more help. It is their strong recommendation that you appoint at least three additional teachers and five parents to the existing committee. You decide to:

A. Suggest that they seek additional part-time help, with the understanding that the people they select will not be regular committee members.

B. Ask for a few days to consider their request.

C. Honor their request.

D. Refuse their request with the explanation that it will make the committee too large.

All of us have dealt with these and similar situations while working in organizational settings. In all such situations, effective decisions must be made if the organization and its members are to function in productive ways. When effective decisions are made, the organization flourishes. When ineffective decisions are made, the organization tends to flounder, and in extreme situations ceases to function at all.

In the previous exercise, what were the answers you chose? If you selected 1-C, 2-B, 3-D, 4-C, and 5-A, you probably chose effective solutions. Notice the term "probably" is used here. Making decisions on complex issues involves probability. There is not always *the* right decision. For example, in our exercise most or even all of the choices offered for each issue could be right in different situations.

In this fastback, information will be offered to show why answers 1-C, 2-B, 3-D, 4-C, and 5-A were probably the most effective solutions for the five situations. Information also will be presented that will explain why the other alternatives would usually be less effective.

Make the Right Decision the First Time

There is one thing that all of us can be sure of concerning decision making: making a decision will be followed immediately by the need to make another decision. In fact, our entire lives involve making one decision after another. Even when we choose not to make a decision, we have made a decision. What is important is making the right decision the first time. If we do not, we are unlikely to achieve the desired result; and we must expend considerable energy undoing the effects of the inadequate decision.

To emphasize this point, consider a learning task such as cursive handwriting. Most second-grade children can learn cursive handwriting if they have a competent handwriting teacher. However, suppose that a decision was made to appoint a second-grade teacher who was incompetent in teaching cursive writing. The children in this teacher's classroom will not only likely lag behind those in other second-grade classes but will also develop many poor handwriting habits. Succeeding handwriting teachers will be required to help these children break many bad habits before they can help them develop more advanced handwriting skills. As a result of the poor initial learning experience, the time required by the children to learn handwriting will be increased, the cost to the school in time and materials will be increased, and the children may never overcome the initial handicap.

Decision-Making Processes

Most authorities consider decision making to be the essence of the administrative process. The quality of the decision-making processes determines the ultimate success of the organization. Decision-making processes may be placed on a continuum from highly rational to highly irrational. This chapter will review two of the most common decision-making processes utilized by organizations and individuals, one being the highly rational process and the other a modification of the rational process.

The Rational Decision-Making Process

The rational decision-making process is the ideal decision-making model. The process is relatively systematic, involves five to ten steps, and in many ways parallels the scientific method. The major assumption behind the process is that any number of people working on a given problem and using the same inputs will arrive at the same solution. Because the rational decision-making process involves sequential steps, it readily lends itself to analysis of each step taken in arriving at a decision. Through analysis the process is refined and upgraded constantly. As individuals gain practice in using the process, their decision-making skills improve over a period of time.

The number of steps in the rational decision-making process may vary depending on the particular model. A compendium of the steps included in the process includes the following:

1. Identify or recognize the problem.
2. Describe, analyze, and evaluate the problem.

3. Collect information pertinent to the problem.
4. Identify alternatives for action.
5. Evaluate alternatives.
6. Select the preferred alternative and implement it.
7. Evaluate the decision.

An elaboration of each of these seven steps follows. For illustrative purposes, we shall use a hypothetical public middle school.

1. *Identify or recognize the problem.*

A new middle school was opened this fall in Happy Valley, U.S.A. The school has eight sections of sixth grade. Most of the sixth-grade teachers in the new school were previously teachers in other upper elementary schools in Happy Valley. In their previous schools, the teachers had a daily class schedule of six fixed periods. Under the six-period schedule, each teacher had four classes, one planning period, and one homeroom period. When the teachers arrived at the new school they found that an eight-period schedule had been implemented by the principal for the current school year. Each teacher now had five class periods, one planning period, one homeroom period, and one general duty period.

During the first six weeks of school the teachers became increasingly dissatisfied with the eight-period schedule. However, the principal was familiar and comfortable with the eight-period schedule and did not feel that there was a real problem. A few brave teachers approached the principal individually to discuss their dissatisfactions; but the principal tactfully ignored their comments, although he did express concern that they were not pleased with the schedule. In late October a group of four teachers formally approached the principal to express their concerns jointly. At this point the principal began to realize the magnitude of the teachers' concerns, but he still refused to modify the schedule. In mid-November the sixth-grade teachers filed a formal grievance with the superintendent of Happy Valley School District. At this point the principal, for the first time, recognized clearly that he had a problem.

2. *Describe, analyze, and evaluate the problem.*

On receipt of the grievance filed by the sixth-grade teachers, the superintendent ordered the teachers and principal to meet and confer about the scheduling problem. During the ensuing conferences the problem became increasingly well defined. The teachers had one additional class period, less in-school planning time, and a period that was not well defined. At this point the superintendent formed a committee to address the issue. The committee consisted of the sixth-grade teachers, the principal, two parents, a member of the teachers association, and a member of the principals association.

3. *Collect information pertinent to the problem.*

The committee now took the initiative and asked parents, students, teachers, and administrators to respond to a questionnaire. It became clear after collecting and interpreting the questionnaire that a majority of the parents and students liked the five class periods because students could take an elective that they had not been able to take previously. Respondents were not particularly committed to the general duty period. The data also indicated that teachers needed more time for preparation and they had less in-school time in which to prepare for classes.

4. *Identify alternatives for action.*

The committee generated a number of alternatives designed to alleviate the scheduling problem. The alternatives ranged from returning to the six-period schedule to maintaining the eight-period schedule. Teachers pushed for fewer preparations, more planning time, and elimination of the general duty period. The principal definitely wanted to keep the five class periods because of favorable parent and student reactions. He also was still not ready to give up the general duty period.

5. *Evaluate alternatives.*

Once the alternatives had been developed and articulated, the committee met several times and developed a procedure for evaluating each alternative based on its potential educational value for students and the cost in terms of human and material resources.

6. *Select the preferred alternative and implement.*

After all of the alternatives were presented and evaluated, the committee selected an alternative that included keeping the five class periods, giving the teachers an extended planning period, and establishing a rotating schedule for the general duty period. The modifications were adopted formally and implemented during the spring semester.

7. *Evaluate the decision.*

A new committee was formed by the superintendent in the early spring and charged with evaluating the decision. A formal evaluation incorporating feedback from major subsystems was requested as a part of the evaluation process. The committee also was charged to prepare and present a final report at the end of the spring semester.

The situation just described is not all that hypothetical. Similar situations frequently occur in schools. Think of the time and effort that could have been saved had there been a good decision-making process in place before the beginning of the school year. A good decision-making process would have mandated a broader participation for developing something as important as a new schedule. Even with broader participation, problems would probably still have arisen; but most likely they would not be of the same magnitude as in the situation just described.

The Modified Rational Decision-Making Process

In actual practice most of us tend to use a modified rational decision-making process. With the modified process, there is little time and effort spent identifying and analyzing a problem. Instead, the problem is only fuzzily defined and we move directly to the solution phase. In doing this, we usually select a solution based on our previous experiences and perceptions. If our decision is reasonably successful, we tend to stop at this stage. However, if our decision is not successful, we often regress to the data-gathering stage, usually to seek those data that will support our hastily selected solution. Having made a decision about a problem, it is difficult to accept data that contradict our solution. As leaders gain more experience, they tend to move away from this short-cut process and toward the more systematic rational decision-making model.

Nonroutine and Routine Decision Making

Decisions can be classified as nonroutine and routine. Nonroutine decision making involves decisions that are complex, occur infrequently, and often involve high risk. High risk are those types of decisions that, if not resolved satisfactorily, result in some form of penalty to those who made the decisions. Nonroutine decisions are too complex to be resolved by referring to a policy statement in a manual or memo; they usually require time and careful deliberation by individuals or groups of people who will be affected by the decision.

Nonroutine Decision Making

It is with nonroutine decision making that the rational decision-making process can best be utilized. Consider the following hypothetical school situation.

Happy Valley School District has three high schools. One of them is Happy Daze High School, which has traditionally been considered a peaceful school with high-achieving students. This year attendance boundary lines were redrawn, which resulted in many students from different socioeconomic backgrounds coming to the school for the first time. With this new mix of students came a dramatic increase in fighting among students. Because of these fights, teachers, parents, and students became very concerned. As the level of concern increased, the principal realized that direct action must be taken quickly.

The principal could treat this as a routine problem and issue a mandate such as, "Any student involved in a fight, for any reason, will automatically be suspended from school for three days." This mandate might work. But suppose it fails. Suppose the principal suspends a number of students for fighting and the parents of the suspended students petition the central office and charge discrimination against their children. If the central office heeds the parents' petition and overrules the principal's decision, the principal's authority will be compromised, thus making the problem even more difficult to solve in the future.

But suppose the principal takes the rational decision-making approach. Here, the principal might decide to create a committee of parents, teachers, administrators, and students to address the problem. Using the rational model, the committee might:

1. Identify and define the problem. Questions such as the following might be raised:
   A. How pervasive is the problem?
   B. Who is primarily affected by the problem?
   C. Are a particular group of students involved?

2. Collect and access appropriate data. Data such as the following might surface:
   A. Two intensely rival groups are now attending the same school for the first time and are involved in most of the fighting.
   B. The fighting stems from previous turf battles and has little to do with the school itself.

3. Generate alternative solutions such as the following:
   A. Bus routes should be rearranged.
   B. Certain students should be assigned to different classes.
   C. Parents of children involved in the fighting should be made aware of their child's involvement.
   D. A social worker should be hired to work with the students involved in the fighting.

4. Select an alternative or alternatives and implement.

5. Evaluate the decision based on the degree of success the school has in reducing or eliminating the fighting.

When dealing with complex, infrequently occuring problems, those in authority should use the rational decision-making process in order to arrive at a solution that is best for all concerned.

Routine Decision Making

Routine decision making is called for in situations that occur frequently and that can be dealt with quickly by using procedures that have been set forth in school board policy statements, building-level regulations, student conduct codes, or school handbooks. For example, a comprehensive school handbook that contains procedures for dealing with routine decisions relieves an administrator or teacher from having to handle every problem on an individual basis. Developing a school handbook initially requires a lot of work; but once developed, it serves as a guide for resolving dozens of routine problems.

Once a well-developed, routine decision-making process has been implemented, a decision maker can deal quickly and automatically with a given issue and go on to other business. However, even well-functioning procedures that are developed for routine decisions must be reviewed on a regular basis, because the longer a particular procedure is in use the more likely situations might change, thereby requiring the modification or deletion of the existing procedure.

Participation in the Decision-Making Process

All leaders have considerable power to make a variety of decisions unilaterally. In fact, such power traditionally has been perceived as the prerogative of a formal leader. However, just having the power to make a decision unilaterally does not ensure that a good decision will be made. Furthermore, some formal leaders try to give the impression that they are involving others in the decision-making process, but they guard the process to such an extent that they are essentially making decisions unilaterally.

A case in point is when an administrator invites his staff to work with him on a project and then proceeds to tell them precisely when each phase of the project must be completed, the format for presenting the project, the length of the project, and so on. In such a case, the administrator is guarding the decision-making process so as to make true involvement impossible.

In contrast to the above authoritarian approach, experienced administrators find that better results are attained by involving subordinates in various stages of the decision-making process. With such involvement, subordinates are likely to assume more responsibility for the project; their contributions will generally be more creative; and they will usually exhibit better attitudes toward the project and the administrator. Successful leaders spend more time seeing that others are appropriately involved in the decision-making process than in making decisions unilaterally.

Two other aspects of decision making are 1) whom to involve in a particular decision-making activity, and 2) when to involve them.

Herbert Simon has developed a useful decision-making model for determining whom to involve in making a decision and when to involve them. Called the "Zone of Acceptance" model, it is shown in Figure 1.

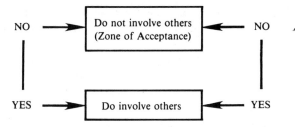

Is the issue relevant to others in the organization?　　**Do others in the organization have expertise to deal with the issue?**

NO ──→ Do not involve others (Zone of Acceptance) ←── NO

YES ──→ Do involve others ←── YES

Figure 1. Simon's model for deciding when to involve others in decision making.

In Simon's model there is a zone in which subordinates are quite willing to accept the decision made by a leader without their input. However, there are other occasions when subordinates would be highly incensed if they were not involved actively in making a decision. The problem for the leader is to determine when a decision affecting subordinates falls within or outside of their zone of acceptance. Two tests are offered to help in determining where a decision falls: the test of relevancy and the test of expertise.

The test of relevancy can be applied by determining if the decision under consideration is relevant to subordinates. If the decision has a direct effect on subordinates or if subordinates are very interested in the decision, then they will want to be included in the decision-making process. If the decision is not relevant to subordinates, then they will usually accept the decision of the leader.

The test of expertise can be applied by determining if subordinates have sufficient expertise to contribute to the decision. If subordinates do not have expertise in an area, involving them in the process probably will lead to frustration or apathy on their part. When subordinates lack expertise, it is usually best for the leader to make decisions without their input.

A decision falls outside the zone of acceptance when subordinates have an interest in and expertise to contribute to that decision.

Therefore, they should be involved in making the decision. Conversely, subordinates having low interest in and little expertise to contribute to a decision fall inside the zone of acceptance and therefore would not want to be involved in making the decision. As in most models of human behavior, there is a grey area. What about subordinates who are not interested but have high expertise, or who are interested but lack expertise?

When subordinates have little expertise to contribute but are interested, it is sometimes useful to involve them so that they know how a decision was made. If they are involved in decision making, even in a limited way, they have a better understanding of the decision and are able to communicate and explain the decision to others.

When subordinates have expertise with respect to an issue that is irrelevant to them, leaders must consider carefully the positive and negative factors of involving them in decision making. For example, when subordinates with expertise already have heavy demands on their time, is it wise to involve them in additional meetings? Or if subordinates have expertise, might they be critical and unsupportive of decisions that were contrary to their informed views? These are only two factors to consider. However, if the subordinates are involved in the process, then they should be included from the earliest stages.

Another procedure leaders may use when trying to decide whether or not to use others in making a decision is a simple checklist. Suppose that an elementary school principal is considering allowing children to enter the school building 10 minutes early during the winter months. Before making such a decision, the principal might wish to determine the possible consequences of the decision on key groups involved: teachers, children, parents, custodial staff, etc. A checklist could be used for this purpose. After each group on the list is a column to indicate their positive and negative reactions to the proposal. The principal using this checklist might find that most teachers oppose the idea of letting children enter school early, most parents would support it, and the children couldn't care less. It would seem that the prudent principal would certainly want to explore the feelings of a number of members of the identified groups before making such a decision.

Speed Versus Accuracy in Decision Making

Speed and accuracy with respect to decision making are not always compatible. A quick decision is not always an accurate one. Unfortunately, during the press of day-to-day activities, many of us forget this fact.

The pressure of time sometimes requires an individual to make a complex decision alone. However, a group will usually make a better decision than an individual. Groups bring a larger pool of knowledge to bear on a particular problem, and through discussion the group tends to sharpen their perceptions of the problem.

What are some ways in which a leader can deal with the problem of speed versus accuracy? First, when a complex problem arises involving a series of decisions, a leader should do everything possible to provide an adequate time for making those decisions. Second, when a leader realizes that a decision must be made in a very short period of time, it is usually best to involve only a small group in the decision-making process. But keep in mind that group decision making is affected by the factor of time.

If groups are given a limited amount of time, they will usually resort to voting in making decisions. In its simplest form this technique involves putting a motion on the floor with the issue being decided by the majority. While this process is quick and relatively conflict free, it usually yields the least desirable decision.

If a moderate amount of time is provided, groups will usually resort to compromise in which individuals or subgroups allow the opposition to have its way with respect to certain decisions, providing they have their way with other decisions. This process will usually provide for a better solution than voting.

Where other factors are equal and groups are given sufficient time, they will reach the best decision through the process of consensus. In this process all individuals and subgroups continue to explore alternatives until they develop one that is mutually acceptable. However, in practice, there tends to be some degree of compromise working in the consensus process.

Even when leaders are able to provide groups with plenty of time, they should consider the composition of the group. Groups composed of individuals less familiar with one another seem to make decisions more quickly but less accurately than well-established groups. One reason for this is that newer groups resort to using voting and compromise techniques more than established groups do. Established groups have a better chance of achieving consensus because they have already established a rapport and are not as concerned about dealing with conflict.

Some Other Decision-Making Techniques

$\mathbf{M}$uch of the literature on decision making employs highly technical approaches that require specialized personnel or complex computer simulations. Most school districts do not have these resources readily available. Fortunately, there are numerous techniques and processes that are relatively inexpensive, simple to use, and readily available to school decision makers. A review of several of these decision-making techniques follows.

Identifying, Describing, and Analyzing a Problem

The need to identify, describe, and analyze a problem constitutes the first part of the rational decision-making model. On the surface these appear to be relatively simple; however, experience shows that this is not the case. Decision makers often spend a considerable amount of time trying to identify what they perceive to be a problem only to find that they have missed the real issue. The technique known as force-field analysis has been found to be useful for problem identification and analysis.

Force-field analysis (Sanders 1977) is a technique that provides a graphic means for dissecting a problem into its component parts. This technique may be used by an individual or a group. The concept is based on the assumption that every situation is in a state of equilibrium as a result of the interaction of a complex field of forces that work in varying directions and at differing strengths. An illustration of the concept is presented in Figure 2.

Force-field analysis postulates two sets of forces in opposition that tend to maintain a given level of activity or output. Sanders identifies these forces as "driving" and "restraining" forces. Driving forces aid in changing the existing level to a new level, while restraining forces tend to maintain the original level and resist change. To move from the existing

Restraining Forces

Existing level ↘ ↘ ↘ ↘ ↘ | ➔ ➔ ➔ ↘   Sought after level

Driving Forces

Figure 2. Force-field analysis.

level to the sought after level involves reducing the restraining forces or increasing the driving forces.

The individual or group using force-field analysis must 1) identify and describe the existing situation as accurately as possible; 2) identify and describe the sought after situation as accurately as possible; 3) identify, describe, and measure the restraining forces; and 4) identify, describe, and measure the driving forces. An example of using the technique of force-field analysis follows.

In recent years there has been considerable amount of criticism concerning the poor reading performance of many students at Happy Daze Elementary School. The low reading scores are of particular concern to parents, teachers, and school administrators. The problem has finally reached a point where the principal feels compelled to appoint a committee representative of the various concerned groups to study the problem. At its first meeting the committee decides to employ the force-field analysis concept in addressing the issue.

The first step in applying force-field analysis to poor reading performance involves the identification and description of the existing situation: "The reading scores for Happy Daze Elementary School students are a full year lower than reading scores in the other elementary schools in Happy Valley School District." The second step involves the identification and statement of a goal: "We want to bring reading scores at Happy Daze Elementary School up to the level of the other elementary schools in Happy Valley School District." Identification of restraining and driving forces is undertaken next. Some restraining forces identified are: 1) Happy Daze School is using an outdated reading

26

program, 2) too much time is spent on subjects other than reading, 3) the teachers at Happy Daze are not well trained in teaching reading, and 4) the Happy Daze students need support services that are not needed by other students in the district. Several driving forces are: 1) the Happy Daze parents are concerned, 2) the local school superintendent is concerned, 3) the staff at Happy Daze Middle School claim that pupils they receive from Happy Daze Elementary are poor readers, and 4) the local newspaper recently published an article criticizing the Happy Daze reading program. These forces could be depicted graphically as shown in Figure 3.

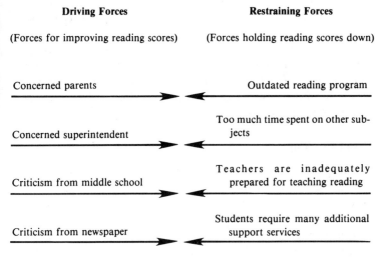

Figure 3. Force-field analysis applied to a school reading problem.

The final step in the process involves shifting the existing equilibrium. This might be accomplished by activities such as installing a new reading program, spending more time during the school day on reading and related activities, involving the teachers in an intensive in-service reading program, and providing support services for the special needs of students at Happy Daze Elementary School.

Once the new goal is achieved, a new equilibrium is established between driving and restraining forces. Constant monitoring of the situation is needed to maintain the new level.

The real advantage of force-field analysis is its simplicity. It can be learned quickly; the user will improve skills in using the technique through experience.

Developing Alternative Solutions to a Problem

Once a problem is known and sufficient data have been collected, the next stage in the rational decision-making process is generating alternative solutions to the problem. Too often this step in the decision-making process does not receive the time and attention it deserves. Once a problem is defined, we usually think of one or two solutions, select one, and then go directly to the implementation stage. With complex problems, a better decision could be reached if a wider range of possible solutions is generated before any solution is selected and implemented. The techniques presented next are particularly effective for generating a variety of solutions to a problem.

Brainstorming

Brainstorming is a decision-making technique that was developed during the 1950s and still is used frequently in many organizations. Properly employed, it is a technique for generating alternative solutions to a problem that can be very useful to decision makers. Essentially, brainstorming involves charging a small group of decision makers to develop as many alternative solutions as possible to a particular problem in a given amount of time.

During the first stage of brainstorming, attempts to discuss the alternatives and to reach a consensus are not permitted. Instead, the emphasis is on generating as wide a range of alternatives as possible. Only after all possible alternatives have been presented should a discussion of the alternatives be initiated.

There are two major criticisms of brainstorming. One criticism involves the effects of peer pressure. Unless the leader is skillful, a few outspoken members begin to dominate the group and reduce input from other members. The second criticism is that after the initial set of alternatives has been generated by the group, a few alternatives begin to emerge as being the best possibilities. As this happens, group members become increasingly hesitant to bring forth new alternatives, and potentially novel alternative solutions to the problem are eliminated from consideration. In practice, the brainstorming process usually generates only a small number of alternatives, and these alternatives tend to be similar.

The Nominal Group Technique

To combat some of the weaknesses in the brainstorming technique, Delbecq and Van de Ven designed the nominal group technique, in which individuals work on a given problem in the presence of one another but do not interact initially. In this process, a small group of decision makers is convened just as they are for brainstorming. The group leader explains the problem to the group and instructs each member to write as many alternative solutions to the problem as possible. Group members are given a set period of time, usually 10 to 20 minutes, and discussion is not permitted during this phase. Once the time period has elapsed, a very structured presentation of alternatives follows. Each member of the group gives one alternative at a time to the group leader, who writes them on a board or large chart. No discussion of the alternatives is permitted until all of the alternatives are recorded.

Research presented by Delbecq and Van de Ven indicates that groups using the nominal group technique generate a larger number of ideas, and ideas of a higher quality, than those produced by brainstorming. They cite several reasons for the superiority of this technique, including:

1. Individuals are not as able to dominate the process as they usually are in brainstorming.

2. The expression of divergent and incompatible ideas is encouraged.

3. Individuals are aware that others are working and know their own work will be displayed. This produces a creative tension among individuals.

Reaching Agreement in Decision Making

Optimally, the best decision will be reached when everyone involved in making the decision agrees. In this situation everyone would be supportive of the decision and assume responsibility for making the decision work. Unfortunately, complete consensus on a complex decision occurs rarely. Therefore, leaders must operate within realistic constraints.

Forced Choices

When leaders find that consensus is not possible, they still need to give the group a sense of direction. One way of doing this is the forced-choices technique.

For an example of the forced-choices technique, consider a situation in which an elementary school principal decides to develop and prioritize a set of instructional goals for her school by using maximum school and community inputs. If the principal establishes a committee including hundreds of parents, students, and teachers to reach consensus on this task, they would probably meet for eternity without reaching true consensus. Instead, as a realistic alternative, the principal might establish a representative committee of parents, teachers, and students to develop a set of instructional goals. The smaller committee will be more likely to reach a consensus on a list of goals. This list of goals could be placed on a survey form and sent to every member of the school community, who would identify four subjects they consider to be most important, four subjects they consider to be moderately important, and four subjects they consider to be least important. The data would then be compiled to determine which goals have the most support. These goals would give a sense of direction to the instructional program.

This forced-choices technique has been used effectively for many years with the Phi Delta Kappa Educational Planning Model, a program used with community groups in setting educational goals for a school system.

Compromise

In the previous situation where a questionnaire was sent to members of the school community, suppose that approximately one-third of the respondents stated that they wanted a traditional curriculum, another third voiced a strong desire for a humanistic curriculum, and the final third called for a career-oriented curriculum.

If the forced-choice procedure fails to provide a clear direction, the principal might want to use the compromise approach.

Once the principal decides to use a compromise approach, the first step would be to convene a new steering committee made up of representatives of all interested groups. After the committee is established, it is important for it to define its purposes. This might involve defining the general purposes of the school (meeting federal and state mandates for example), defining the particular types of curriculum emphasis each group desired, and determining the resources available to the school. After defining the committee's purposes, it probably would become clear to all concerned that the school has limited resources and cannot be all things to all people. The committee then could concentrate on working out a compromise that is acceptable to all concerned. One compromise scenario might be a new program with all students spending approximately two-thirds of the school day in a common set of core courses. For the remainder of the day the school could be divided into three "schools within a school," with each school having its own curriculum emphasis. Students and parents could then choose the curriculum emphasis in which they are most interested.

Reaching Consensus

The optimum decisions usually are reached through consensus. Reaching consensus in decision making is also the most difficult level to achieve. Although it requires additional time and effort, a consensus decision is usually a higher quality decision than one made through voting or compromise. The extra time it takes in reaching consensus is probably far less than the time and effort it would take to undo a bad decision.

There are a number of factors that leaders and group members should consider when attempting to reach consensus on an issue:

1. Ensure that the group has adequate time and material resources available.
2. Gather as many pertinent facts as possible before trying to reach any type of closure.
3. Avoid early attempts to compromise.
4. Committee members should resist changing their positions as long as their positions are valid and rational.
5. Listen to what others are saying and try to understand their position.
6. Some compromises probably will have to be made, but avoid compromise until it is absolutely necessary.

Synthesis

For discussion purposes, several decision-making techniques were presented above as separate entities. In practice, these techniques usually are used in conjunction with one another, as illustrated in the following examples:

1. The initial step in the decision-making process involves becoming aware of a problem. This step is particularly difficult to accomplish in large organizational settings. Therefore, a leader might begin by getting input from a few key people. The brainstorming technique can be useful for this purpose.

2. Defining and analyzing a problem is the second step in the decision-making process. A technique such as force-field analysis can be very useful for understanding the various components of a problem.

3. For the developing alternatives step in the decision-making process, the nominal group technique has proven to be effective.

4. For the step involving selection from alternatives, the forced-choices, compromise, and consensus techniques are useful.

5. For the implementation step in the process, the consensus-building techniques can be used to arrive at the many decisions involved in carrying out a project.

Conclusion

Making good decisions is the essence of leadership. And since educators assume many different leadership roles, regardless of the official title they hold, they are involved in making decisions — important decisions affecting the education of boys and girls. Awareness of the process of rational decision making and of techniques to carry out that process should result in better decisions. This has been the purpose of this fastback.

Bibliography

Bridges, Edwin M. "A Model for Shared Decision-Making in the School Principalship." *Educational Administration Quarterly* 3 (Fall 1968): 51.

Delbecq, Andre L., and Van de Ven, Andrew H. "A Group Process Model for Problem Identification and Program Planning." *Journal of Applied Behavioral Science* 7 (Summer 1971): 466-92.

George, Claude S. *The History of Management Thought*. Englewood Cliffs, N.J.: Prentice-Hall, 1972.

Gore, William J. "Decision-Making Research: Some Prospects and Limitations." In *Concepts and Issues in Administration Behavior*, edited by Sidney Maileck and Edward Van Ness. Englewood Cliffs, N.J.: Prentice-Hall, 1962.

Kimbrough, Ralph B., and Nunnery, Michael Y. *Educational Administration: An Introduction*. New York: Macmillan Publishing Co., 1976.

Kline, John A. *Practical Techniques for Achieving Consensus*. A study at Maxwell Air Force Base, 1974.

Pharis, William L., et al. *Decision-Making and Schools for the 70's*. Washington, D.C.: National Education Association Center for the Study of Instruction (CSI), 1970.

Sanders, Stanley G. "Force-Field Analysis: A Functional Management System." *Planning and Changing* 7 (Winter 1977): 143, 144.

Simon, Herbert A. *Administrative Behavior*. New York: The Macmillan Co., 1947.